CATCH
Every Ball

CATCH *Every Ball*

HOW TO HANDLE LIFE'S PITCHES

JOHNNY BENCH
with Paul Daugherty

ORANGE FRAZER PRESS
Wilmington, Ohio

ISBN 978-1933197-12-8
Copyright © 2008 Johnny Bench
www.johnnybench.com

Copies of *Catch Every Ball: How to Handle Life's Pitches*
may be ordered directly from:

Orange Frazer Press
P.O. Box 214
Wilmington, OH 45177

1.800.852.9332
www.orangefrazer.com

Cover design by Chad DeBoard and Jeff Fulwiler
Book design by Chad DeBoard

Second Printing

Library of Congress Cataloging-in-Publication Data

Bench, Johnny, 1947-
  Catch every ball : how to handle life's pitches / by Johnny Bench,
with Paul Daugherty.
       p. cm.
  ISBN 978-1-933197-12-8
  1. Success. 2. Management. I. Daugherty, Paul, 1957- II. Title.
  BF637.S8B447 2008
  650.1--dc22
                          2008012390

DEDICATION & THANKS

To my parents, Ted and Katy, my brothers, Teddy and William, and my sister, Marilyn. To the people of Oklahoma, especially Binger, the root of it all. To all of my managers, coaches, and the teammates who made me better. To my son Bobby—you make me proud. And to Lauren, who came into my life and made it totally complete, and gave me Justin. I love you all.

Thank you to Reuven Katz, who has guided me through my professional life both on and off the field. Thank you to my many friends, in business and in golf, for sharing your days and laughter with me. And thank you Paul and Marcy, who helped to make this book possible.

TABLE OF CONTENTS

I was at the podium, fumbling.

Catchers have to be in control—of their pitchers, the game, themselves. I could hit and throw as well as any catcher who ever played baseball. But there was more to it than that. I had to be in charge. When I was behind the plate, there was never a doubt who was running things on the field, which made my bumbling appearance at the National 4-H Convention all the more embarrassing.

This was 15 years ago, at least. I'd been asked to speak to a group of 6,000 in Kansas City. I was comfortable with public appearances. I'd played 17 years, appeared on national TV, and toured the world with Bob Hope. Center stage suited me.

Normally, I'd ad-lib my way through speeches. On this day, because the crowd was so large, I wanted to give them something extra. I decided to write the speech. What resulted was a rambling, disjointed mess. I'd depart from the script for an anecdote, then try to come back to it. I'd pause. To me, pauses reveal a lack of direction. The speech didn't work. I wasn't decisive. I knew what I wanted to say, but the delivery was so off, I never got it said.

Right after I finished, I knew it was bad, and I knew how to fix it. I'd heard speakers make their points using the letters of the alphabet. I'd always thought 26 points were about 21 too many for people to recall and process. I settled on the five vowels. Vowels are action letters. My message has always been to take action when living your life. I called them the Vowels of Success.

The Vowels have become the core of my message. In the past 15 years, I've made thousands of speeches to organizations and companies. I've been a spokesman for numerous products. I'm on the road more than 250 days a year, hoping to inspire people in their careers and their personal lives, provoking thought and discussion on how to do and be better.

My Vowels are fluid. They change over time, they bend to the situations I face. Your principles shouldn't change; the actions that guide them are flexible. The point is, don't let life happen to you. Take control.

As you read this book, I'd ask you to formulate your own Vowels. Assign a few Vowels to each chapter. You'd be surprised at how easy it is to organize your thoughts and turn them into actions. In the last chapter, I've given you my Vowels. The appendix includes the Vowels of many friends and people I admire.

If you take one thought from this book, I hope it's one of these:

You are important. Rely on yourself. Become someone upon whom others rely, as well. All of us have areas in which we can excel. It's up to you to find your excellence and take advantage of it. Believe in yourself. Don't expect others to do it for you. Take control. Catch every ball.

—Johnny Bench
June 2008

CATCH
Every Ball

Mine was no rags-to-riches story. I grew up in Binger, Oklahoma, a tiny town in the eastern half of the state, about an hour from Oklahoma City. I was successful at everything I tried. Sports? I was all-state in basketball and baseball. Schoolwork? I was the valedictorian of my high school graduating class. Baseball? I batted .600 as a high school sophomore. As a pitcher, I never lost a game in my life until the state high school playoffs my sophomore year, and that was 2–1 on a passed ball.

The Cincinnati Reds drafted me out of high school at age 17. At 19, I was a starting catcher in the major leagues. Three years later, in 1970, I was the National League's Most Valuable Player, on a team that won 70 of its first 100 games and went to the World Series.

I batted cleanup for arguably the best team ever assembled. You can't think of the Big Red Machine without seeing me behind the plate. By the time I was 21, I'd been the league's best player and traveled the world with Bob Hope. I'd sat next to Henry Kissinger at a state dinner. I'd played golf with Arnold Palmer. By 1970, I was making $20,000 a year, but leading the life of a king.

Why should anyone listen to me?

It starts with a school bus, going down a 45-degree hill on State Route 281 four miles east of Binger, on April 1, 1965. There was a half mile of two lanes between the top of the hill and the guardrail at the bottom, where 281 ended in a T at Route 152.

Sometimes, life turns forever on the most insignificant of moments. We'd just won a baseball game at Riverside Indian School and were headed back to Binger. Our coach, Lloyd Dinse, was behind the wheel. One of our teammates, Spud Domebo, lived at the top of the hill, but he'd been sick that day, so we didn't need to stop to let him off. If we had, coach Dinse would have known the brakes weren't working.

We were halfway down the hill when Lloyd Dinse started tapping the brake pedal and got no response. His foot pushed the pedal to the floor. "Boys," he said, "we're out of brakes."

"April Fools!" I shouted. Less than a minute later, two of my teammates were dead.

The bus, loaded with ballplayers, slammed the

guardrail at the T intersection at 50 miles an hour.
A couple hundred feet from the guardrail, Dinse
had tried to turn left, but the bus was going too fast.
It flipped three times before settling upright in the
red Oklahoma dust. My feet hung out the back
emergency exit. David Gunter lay beneath me. I'd
saved both our lives.

My dad, Ted Bench, drove a propane gas truck for
a living. I'd gone with him numerous times. When I
was 11 or 12, one of dad's drivers, James Costello, had
made a run in bitterly cold weather. He was running
propane from the refinery to supply the irrigation
wells used on farms around Binger. James' windshield
froze over. He couldn't see the slick of ice on the road.
He crashed and died. After that, Ted Bench said to
me, "If you're ever in a wreck get low, down on the
floorboards," he told me. As our school bus began
its crazy, death-ride, I grabbed David Gunter and
smothered him beneath a seat.

I saw my friend Jerry Scott, holding on to a bar
near the front of the bus. Jerry was swinging on the
bar, one time around every time the bus flipped. He
looked like the red and white stripes on a barber pole.

The crash took an eternity, even as it lasted just
a few seconds. Imagine yourself being tumbled in the
world's largest dryer. We all crawled out of the bus
when it stopped. It was the strangest silence I've ever

heard, if that makes sense.

Everyone was moving around, except Billy Wiley and Harold Dean Sims, a couple of reserves on the team. Billy had been thrown from the bus and run over by one of the rear tires. Harold suffered massive head injuries. We buried them a week later. I was 17. All I'd suffered was a spike mark on my right elbow.

Terrible things happen to all of us.

A year later, I was playing minor league ball. I'd broken my thumb near the end of the season, so they sent me home. I was driving on a four-lane highway between Wichita, where my brother lived, and Binger. It was late at night when I pulled out from the right lane to pass a semi-truck. I didn't see the drunk driver in time.

He was driving the wrong way. I hit my brakes and pulled hard to the right. He hit me broadside. My car folded into a V shape. Incredibly, a doctor was driving the car that was following me that night. He called for help. I didn't come to until they put me in the ambulance. My first thought was, "Please God, don't let me die. Mom and Dad will be so disappointed." I was in the hospital a few days, without so much as a broken bone.

Two of my good friends weren't so lucky. Spud Domebo was a 5-foot-8, 185-pound shortstop who was fast and had a great glove. Spud had joined the Army after high school graduation, where he'd set the base record for the mile run in combat boots. I came home from winter ball after my first year as a professional and said, "You're better than lots of guys I play with. I have to get you a tryout." Two days later Spud, who had missed the bus wreck because he hadn't made the trip to Anadarko, fell asleep at the wheel while driving, slammed into a culvert and died.

Then there was Danny Lopez, yet another high school teammate. Danny enlisted in the Army after graduation. He went to Vietnam and earned several medals for bravery. After his discharge, Danny came home to Binger, where he went to work driving a delivery truck. One day he was driving on the two-lane when an elderly woman pulled out from behind a cotton trailer and hit him head on. He died instantly.

By the time I was 19 years old, I'd experienced the deaths of four high school teammates. Death informs us all, especially when we are young and see dying as a concept, a mist in some far, distant fog. I learned very early, too early perhaps, that life is precarious. It's why I don't spend much time pondering what I can't control.

"Don't waste a worry" is what I'd tell my mother, Katy Bench. "Everything will work out."

I don't mean to sound callous. The deaths of Billy,

Harold, Danny, and Spud affected me profoundly. I took something from them, though: We have to put things aside. Self-pity doesn't accomplish anything, and it doesn't matter what happened the day before. You have a responsibility to yourself and others to perform. It's game time, every day. You have to play.

Why listen to Johnny Bench?

It was early September 1972, the Reds were in a pennant race and I was having a very good year. I felt fine; the spot on my lung was discovered during a routine physical all the players underwent each September. Mentally, it covered me like a shroud. I played the rest of the season without knowing exactly what was wrong with me.

In one stretch, I hit seven home runs in seven days. I won the National League home run title. In the playoffs against Pittsburgh, I hit a leadoff home run in the bottom of the 9th inning of the fifth and final game. It tied the score 3-3. The Reds went on to win the game and advance to the World Series.

I still didn't know what was wrong with me, but it was game time. I had to play.

In the offseason, doctors cut me open, peeled back two ribs and discovered what was wrong. They took care of it, but part of me had vanished. I'd never be the player I'd been. Johnny Bench stopped being Johnny Bench, at least the physical person. I became more human.

I also knew there was more to me than baseball. I could still play, but I could also do other things. I spent lots more time talking with people whose success had nothing to do with baseball. I learned from Tom Devlin how to build a business from the ground up. I watched Arnold Palmer charm thousands of people, simply by saying hello and calling them by their first names.

Already, at age 25, the contacts I'd made through baseball served me well. I marveled at the work ethic of Bob Hope, who never put on a bad show. I listened to Frank Sinatra speak of the importance of being on time. Everything you take from someone can be replaced. Everything but time.

I became friends with the great college basketball coach Bob Knight. He taught me to flyfish. I stayed close with friends I'd made in Binger. Anyone who has grown up in a small place understands: You might leave the place, but the place never leaves you. Life lessons are more easily digested in a town where time barely moves and everyone knows your name. David Gunter, the boy I pulled to the floor as the bus was tumbling, still lives in Oklahoma. He's the president of Durant Peanut Company.

I used the knowledge of the people I met. Still do.

I'll share all of it in this book.

Why listen to Johnny Bench?

I don't have a Ph.D. I don't even have a college education. I was a catcher. You have to be dumb as a box of rocks to be a catcher. Who wants to spend his entire working life in the dirt, wearing heavy clothing? Catchers don't know anything.

I learned, though. I studied. I started picking cotton when I was 6 years old. In Oklahoma in the 1950s, we started school early in August, so we could take a three-week break in September and October to pick the cotton crop. I'd go to the fields with a jug of water and a scrambled egg sandwich. They'd pay me two cents a pound. I could pick 300 pounds a day, on my knees, no green bolls allowed, no leaves in the sack, hands cut up. With the money I made, I could buy a pair of irregular Levi's.

I chopped weeds from the peanut patches in the summertime. Ninety-five degrees and sunny, every day. By the time I was in 8th grade, I was getting up at 2 in the morning, lifting 90-pound sacks of peanuts into truck beds. I was 5 foot 2, weighed 120 pounds. I'd get the sack to my chest, then up on my head, like a clean and jerk move, then push it into the truck.

At age 15, when I was old enough to drive, I'd drive my dad's propane truck. My dad would get up at 4 a.m., before it got hot, and make all of his deliveries, so he'd have some time later to spend with his family. When I wasn't driving, I'd paint the propane tanks for $3 an hour. I'd crawl under houses with my dad, to learn how plumbing works, or how to set up a gas heater.

The point is, I didn't grow up privileged. I never went to a summer baseball camp. I never had my equipment paid for. The only silver spoons in the Bench household were heirlooms. I'm the catcher on Baseball's All Century Team. I can also fix your gas leak.

Why listen to Johnny Bench?

I've had success and failure at the highest level. I've been married four times. (This time, I got it right. Persistence does matter, in all things.)

I've been around some of the best and brightest, from Donald Trump to Sparky Anderson to Pete Rose. I've seen spectacular success and failure, personally and from those around me. I'm not too good to admit failure and weakness. I'm not too smart to forego learning. I'll never be so wise that I'll stop trying to be wiser.

People interest me. Business interests me. Success interests me, but no more than failure. Winning demands losing, as sure as cotton demands rain. We all make mistakes. The smart among us don't make the same one twice. The Reds went from the World

Series in 1970 to a losing record in 1971. I went from MVP to MDP. Most Valuable to Most Disappointing.

The Reds learned from that, making a few trades and regrouping. I learned, going from a season of boos to hitting 40 homers. We all grew in the process.

I'm not going to tell you in this book what you have to do. I'm going to tell you what you might think about doing. The rest is up to you.

I make my living now giving motivational speeches. The question I get most often is, "My son is a catcher for his team. What's the best advice you can give him?"

"Catch every ball," I say.

I could spend a lot of time lecturing on developing quadricep muscles and working on footwork, tossing the baseball long distances and learning to see the whole field. I could emphasize catching with one hand, the technique I made popular. But really, when people ask me that, I think they're also looking for something a bit more involved.

Catch every ball. Easy to say, hard to do. Catch every ball. Grasp everything life throws, good and bad. Handle it with the fewest number of errors. Pitches come your way every day, in the form of decisions you will make that define who you are. Handle the pitches. When you don't, understand why, so when the next one arrives, you will.

I've handled many pitches in my life. I was the catcher on the best team ever. I was the catcher on the best all star team ever. I know how to handle pitchers. And pitches.

Spend some time with me, in these pages. Catch what I'm throwing. I'm just like you. But I've learned how to catch, perhaps better than most.

LIFELINES

In the spring of 1967 in the Class AAA minor league town of Buffalo, N.Y., pitchers Dom Zanni and Jim Duffalo were hanging around hoping for one more chance. Baseball is a young man's game. If you don't get it right, right away, you spend lots of years working on breaking balls and making impressions.

Zanni was 35 and had spent all or parts of five seasons with three different major league clubs. Duffalo was just 31, but his career was already on the downturn. Each was looking to rediscover that bite at the end of his curveball that made the difference between bus rides and five-star hotels. Each was hoping a major league team would be paying attention if it happened.

As it was, Zanni and Duffalo never pitched in the majors again. They did achieve one thing, though: They helped me become a Hall of Famer.

I was 19 in 1967, and I thought I knew

everything. What I didn't know was how to hit a good curveball. The road to the major leagues is lined with hitters who couldn't hit the curve. Zanni and Duffalo saw something special in me. They took me out to eat. The first bar I ever entered was with those two.

They talked. I listened. It made all the difference.

Kid, we're going to teach you to hit a curveball.

"I could see the potential right away," Zanni recalled recently. "He was such a strong kid. He had such quick hands. He didn't have to swing very hard. He just needed to stay back and be patient. I threw him curveball after curveball, from all angles, over the top, from the side, everywhere."

Zanni asked to room with me on the road, so we could get to the ballpark early. We even worked on it in the bullpen. He'd throw curves, I'd stand there with a bat in my hands and watch the spin on the ball. "You're a catcher," he'd tell me. "You know what pitchers throw. Start thinking like a pitcher."

I'd hit 100 curves a day, every day from April to June. We'd meet each afternoon at 3:30 at War Memorial Stadium in downtown Buffalo, a decaying hulk of a ballpark. "A place that made you want to get back to the big leagues real quick" was how Zanni put it. They filmed the movie "Field of Dreams" there; War Memorial was anything but. It looked as if they'd stuck a baseball field inside a football stadium. You had to hit it into the end zone to get a home run.

A pitching machine couldn't duplicate the speed and the break on a good curve, but Zanni and Duffalo could. They'd appear some 90 minutes before batting practice, with plastic buckets full of baseballs and throw me curve after curve. I was promoted to the Reds in August.

I'd spend the rest of my career as a hitter looking for the curveball first. Most hitters seek out the fastball, then look for the breaking ball. But I'd become so confident in hitting curveballs—hands back, watch the rotation of the baseball, don't commit to the swing too soon—I was able to guess when a curve was coming and either hit it if it "hung" out over the plate, or foul it off until I could feast on a fastball.

If you don't ask questions, you don't learn. Everyone can teach us something. I've learned by listening to Donald Trump, Bob Hope, and Arnold Palmer. I've learned by watching everyday people. Dom Zanni and Jim Duffalo were never going to be good major-leaguers. That didn't mean what they had to say wasn't valuable.

In 1970, three years removed from curveballs with Dom, I was the Most Valuable Player in the National

League, on what would become one of the best teams of all time. I owed some of it to Jim Duffalo and Dom Zanni.

I speak often at corporate awards banquets. I'll tell those present, "If you didn't win an award tonight, talk to someone who did. Ask them how they did it." Don't be afraid to learn. Use the knowledge of others. I've spent my entire adult life asking questions, seeking answers from those I admire, whether they are heads of corporations or the guys who cut my grass. My life is a sponge. I absorb, I squeeze out, I absorb some more.

I didn't know the first thing about studying pitchers when I got to Newport News, Va., in 1966, as a member of the Class A Peninsula Grays. Linc Curtis knew. Curtis was a 25-year-old first baseman, 6-foot-5, built like Adonis, a relaxed southern Californian who was doing what he loved.

He still had the dream, but he knew it drifted further from him with every day he spent in sleepy seaside Virginia. Linc had lived his baseball career in the backwaters of the low minor leagues. He'd say to me, "If I don't do well this year, my baseball career might be over." Linc was right; you can't find his name in any listing of current or former professional ballplayers.

Linc Curtis never played in the majors. That didn't stop him from helping me further my own dream. Linc talked. I listened.

"This guy likes to throw the fastball away," he might say. "Be patient. Keep your hands back."

He was my own personal scouting report. Curtis was always encouraging, like a brother to me. I was young and eager. I was easily frustrated. I had a temper and wanted everything yesterday. I broke so many helmets slamming them on the concrete dugout floor that some weeks, I barely made a paycheck.

At $35 a helmet, I needed to do something. I'd been taking lots of foul tips off the top of my head. Also, the ill-fitting mask I wore would slide sideways every time I made a throw to second base. The crossbar would cut me across the bridge of my nose.

I started wearing the helmet backwards when I was behind the plate. It kept the mask from sliding and prevented foul balls from bruising the top of my head. Plus, I figured if I wanted to wear the helmet while I was catching, I'd better not throw it after a bad at bat. I pioneered the use of a helmet behind the plate.

Meantime, Linc Curtis was keeping me cool.

"Relax. You're gonna be great. You just need to go through this," he'd say. He was right, but I didn't realize it until I heard him say it. We're all fragile. We all need people boosting our confidence, even if we are members of Baseball's All Century Team.

Later that season, I noticed a stack of game notes that the Reds had sent to my manager with the Grays, Pinky May. One note said something like, "Bench could be the next catcher in Cincinnati." A year later, thanks in part to Linc, Dom, and Jim, I was.

If you can't do something, do something about it. Ask. Learn. Be open, be flexible, be curious. Live life with your eyes and ears trained. God gave you two ears and one mouth. Listen twice as much as you talk.

Be a sponge. The people who fail are those who are afraid to ask how or why.

Life is learning to hit a curveball. To learn to hit curves, ask someone who has hit a few, or thrown them. Opportunity comes without notice, tragedy without warning. It's how you handle the twists that makes all the difference.

I watched Bob Hope in the years we did the USO tours in Vietnam and around the world. I learned how a consummate pro does things. We flew around the world in 12 days, on the same plane. Bob had a mattress on the plane, but he didn't sleep much. He was always writing and rewriting. His attitude was, "I'm going to give these guys the best show I can, every day."

I watched Arnold Palmer play golf. I've played with him many, many times. I learned how much the common touch means, especially from an uncommon man. Everywhere he played, Arnold seemed to know half his fans by name. He did something incredibly simple, yet increasingly difficult: Arnold was good to people. He made them feel comfortable, no matter who they were. In my speaking, I've learned from him to do the same.

I watched the great college basketball coach Bob Knight conduct practices. I went flyfishing with him. I learned the necessity of discipline and focus. I heard Knight say something I will never forget:

"Don't tell people what you stand for. Tell them what you won't stand for."

I watched Ted Bench rise every morning at 4 a.m. to deliver propane gas. I learned the nobility of work done well.

I watched Lee Trevino read the break on putts. "That left-to-right putt?" Trevino said. "Play it forward in your stance. The putter blade closes, so the ball stays up the hill. How many times have you hit a putt and it breaks too early? It's because the toe of the putter isn't closing. If you play the ball forward in your stance, you give the toe a little more time to close. If you're putting right to left, put the ball back in your stance."

Time is priceless, but knowledge is free. It demands nothing but your curiosity.

Here's something else: By asking questions, you not only empower yourself by getting answers, you also empower those whose expertise you're seeking.

The 1970 season was Sparky Anderson's first as manager of the Cincinnati Reds. No one knew quite what to make of Sparky, a minor-league manager whose own playing career was nondescript. "That minor-league mother" was what my teammate Lee May called Sparky.

But Sparky knew human nature. He understood we all need to be acknowledged, respected, needed. "Lemme ask you something," Sparky said to me on the dugout steps of the Tampa field we called home in March. It was the first day of spring training. "John, should we use this field for extra hitting? Or do you think that one over there would be better?"

It was a mundane question. I don't even know if Sparky cared which field was used for what. The point was, he'd asked my opinion, sought my advice. This man thinks I'm important enough to consult? For the first time, I felt like a pro, like I had a brain.

That's the way it went with Sparky every year he managed the Reds. He'd call in Joe Morgan, Pete Rose, Tony Perez, and me usually just to take the pulse of the club. He'd ask us about trades, who we thought might fit into our clubhouse mix. In the mid-1970s, Sparky asked me, "John, we have a chance to get Phil Niekro. What do you think?" By then, the legendary knuckleballer was 36 or 37 years old and a .500 pitcher. I didn't think he had a lot left. Plus, catching any knuckleball pitcher required a butterfly net and a body immune to bruises.

"I think you better get his catcher, too," I said.

We didn't get Phil Niekro.

Sparky didn't always listen. But he always asked. In so doing, he made us feel a part of what was going on. If you're hesitant to ask questions, think of it that way. Most of the time, you're honoring the person whose knowledge you seek.

When I arrived in Cincinnati, I didn't know much about investing money. Remember, I grew up in Oklahoma, in a house of modest means. I was a country kid in all ways. Saving was something rich people did. When I made two cents a pound picking cotton, I spent it on blue jeans or a baseball glove.

I met Hy Ullner in Cincinnati. Ullner was a character. He owned Hyde Park Clothing, across the Ohio River from Cincinnati, in northern Kentucky. He was the "Bargain City Kid" who'd made himself rich and locally famous by owning a discount department store called Rink's Bargain City. Hy would appear in TV ads wearing a holster and a six-shooter to "shoot" the screen full of discounts.

"I want to invest some money," I told Hy.

"What do you like?" he asked, not unlike Warren Buffett. "That's what you should buy."

This was 1970. I was making around $20,000 when Hy put me on a budget to start saving. Whatever my rent and expenses were, he gave me the same amount for an allowance. I was MVP in 1970 and got a new contract for $40,000. Appearances and commercials gave me another $20,000 or so. I made a commercial for Wheaties for $7,500 where I mishandled a bunt, struck out and then on a pop-up near the stands a fan reached out and caught the ball, dropped it into my mitt and said, "Hey Johnny, you should have had your Wheaties." I wouldn't have done it again for $100,000. All I heard for the next few years was "Hey Johnny, you didn't have your Wheaties." You can imagine it was quite a lot when as a player you only succeed about 30 percent of the time.

Anyway, I was putting the money into the bank and I was on my way to being rich as far as Binger was concerned. When did I get to $75,000, I'm not sure, but I would guess it was by 1971 or '72. I made $80,000 after my second MVP season. That was 1973.

I have a friend from Wichita, Kansas, named Tom Devlin who taught me that asking questions is vital; just as important is knowing who to ask. It's about who you surround yourself with. If you're associated with known felons, you're probably going to learn to break into a house. If you surround yourself with smart, passionate people, some of their success is bound to rub off.

Hy Ullner got me started; Tom Devlin advanced the process immeasurably.

Tom didn't have much money initially, but he had a vision and a plan: Create a business where people who needed a tool or an appliance, once or occasionally—a chainsaw for a downed tree, say, or a power washer to clean a deck or siding, a post-hole digger—could rent the equipment rather than buy it.

He needed $25,000 to get started, $10,000 of which he borrowed from his mother. His mother borrowed the money, using her house as security. A while ago, Tom Devlin sold his business, Rent-A-Center, for $580 million.

Tom only invests in things he knows about. It's the same advice Hy Ullner offered me in 1970. Tom wants a business he knows from bottom to top, so if something goes wrong, he knows how to fix it.

In 2004, I was asked to appear on the hit TV show "Who Wants to Be a Millionaire." You might recall, it was a quiz show in which questions got progressively more difficult as the dollar amount increased. Contestants were allowed "Lifelines," options for obtaining additional help. One lifeline was called

Phone A Friend. Before going on the show, you'd designate five acquaintances whose expertise you trusted.

It seems odd that a TV game show can offer such a simple life lesson, but that one did: Surround yourself with accomplished people. Don't hesitate to ask about what you don't know.

I chose George Schaefer, then the CEO of Fifth Third Bank in Cincinnati, if I had a financial question. I tapped my friend Cal Levy, who once managed the rock star Prince, for pop culture help. My attorney, Reuven Katz, would handle a legal query, Erich Kunzel, the conductor for the Cincinnati Pops Orchestra, had the music angle covered. Finally, another friend, Greg LaLonde would be my guru when it came to overall knowledge.

I called LaLonde to answer this question: "Every Corvette sports car in America is made in what state?" LaLonde knew it was Kentucky. I won $250,000 for The Johnny Bench Scholarship Fund of the Greater Cincinnati Foundation with that answer. I hit that curveball out of the park, because I wasn't afraid to ask for help, and I knew the right people to ask.

Dom Zanni and Jim Duffalo would be proud.

PITCHERS ARE PEOPLE, TOO.

We all have an obligation to share our talents, to lift others with the power of who we are. If we don't, we're squandering half of what we've been given. It could be as simple as a word of thanks. It could be more than that. With a guy like Clay Carroll, it was a matter of showing him confidence and appreciation. He came to know we believed in him and depended on him. Everyone who thrives needs that. He took it from there.

At age 66, Clay Palmer Carroll remains the best-known native son of Clanton, Ala., population 7,800, halfway between Birmingham and Montgomery on Interstate 65. Other than Carroll, Clanton is known for producing peaches, enough that the town's water tower bears the shape of a peach.

The best day of Carroll's life, he figures, was June 5, 1968, the day the Atlanta Braves traded him to the

Cincinnati Reds. He went from a bad team to a team on the rise. And he had me as a catcher.

There is absolutely no difference between how a catcher handles his pitching staff and how a supervisor handles his employees. You know your people. You challenge them to be better than they think they can be. You make them feel special. You set a standard and expect it to be met.

How do you do that? You build trust. You let your people know all you're trying to do is get their best. The rapport I established with pitchers is the same a boss should author with his workers. Once a pitcher knew I had taken the time to know his personality and the way he liked to pitch, he was much more open to taking direction from me. You can't merely tell people what to do. You also have to tell them why.

As Sparky Anderson put it, "The difference between a good manager and a great manager is, a good manager will tell you there's more than one way to skin a cat. A great manager will convince the cat it's necessary."

Knowing your employees was a lesson reinforced over and over, in my baseball career and beyond, from Sparky Anderson to Bob Hope. These people had a talent for making you feel special. They took the time to get to know you personally, so they understood what got you going.

For me, dealing with Clay Carroll was no different than dealing with any talented, underachieving employee. When he was with the Braves—"I stunk, the team stunk, we all stunk," he'd say, years later—I knew he had the stuff to be a much better pitcher than he was. With Clay, it was all about confidence.

He was a timid guy on the mound. He pitched scared. When he made a mistake with a pitch and got hit hard, he wouldn't throw it again. When Clay was with the Braves, I called him Sunny Sunoco. As a relief pitcher, his best attribute was pouring gasoline on the fire.

That was about to change. When he came to the Reds, I made him a project. Through the years, so did Pete Rose, Joe Morgan and Tony Perez. We called him "Hawk." One reason was obvious: Carroll had a beak for a nose. Another reason was more subtle: The name gave him a better self-image. In 1988, Los Angeles Dodgers manager Tommy Lasorda began referring to a skinny, concave-chested righthander in his starting rotation as "Bulldog." Orel Hershiser looked like a bulldog as much as a cat resembled an airplane. But Lasorda knew Hershiser could use the boost.

That year, Hershiser pitched a major league-record 59 consecutive scoreless innings. Bulldog won the National League Cy Young Award and the Dodgers stunned the Oakland A's in the World Series.

Whenever Hawk entered a game as a Cincinnati Reds pitcher, I stuck the ball in his glove and said, "You're good at this. This is where I really need you." I'd conclude every session by saying, "You can do it, Hawk." He'd always answer, "I can do it." Only with Clay Carroll from Clanton, Ala., it always came out, "Ah kin dew it."

Sometimes, as with any pitcher, you had to keep Clay focused. You had to grab him verbally by the shirt: "You've got to run this fastball in on this guy, and you've got to do it right now. C'mon, Hawk. You can do it."

"Ah kin dew it."

When he did, you patted him on the back and watched his whole personality change. It was literally a physical thing. His chest swelled. He offered this big, country boy grin. Tony, Pete, Joe and I believed in him. Hawk figured if four future Hall of Famers approved, he must really be something.

"They used to call me "Bring-It," Clay said not too long ago. He's retired now from construction work and living in Soddy Daisy, Tenn., a dot on the map near Chattanooga. If you ask him what goes on in Soddy Daisy, he says, "nothin' but sittin' on your rear."

"Johnny'd give me the ball, call me Hawk, tell me to bring it. I could throw a fastball pretty good. He'd pump me up, make me think I could blow one past Babe Ruth. I'd tell him, 'Just gimme the ball, I'll show you.'"

With his fastball, Hawk ended up breaking more bats than any pitcher we had. Once we started boosting him up, talking about all the bats he broke, he developed a swagger. His talent was obvious; he needed someone to believe in him. In nearly eight years as a Red, he was one of the best relievers we ever had, and among the best in baseball. Clay went from obscurity in Atlanta to winning a World Series in 1975 in Cincinnati. In 1972, he led the National League in saves and games pitched, and finished fifth in the Cy Young balloting. In 32 postseason innings, covering 22 appearances, he had a remarkable 1.39 earned run average.

He became an integral part of the Big Red Machine. Clay Carroll became what we believed he could be.

I saw this over and over. In 1978, we had a young relief pitcher named Tom Hume. Decent fastball and slider, not a lot of confidence. One day that year in Philadelphia, Hume threw a pitch I'd never seen him throw before, a sinker that broke like someone shot it. Straight down and in to a right-handed hitter.

I caught that pitch, called timeout and trotted out to the mound. "He took the ball in his hand and hit me in the chest with it," Hume recalled not long ago. "He said, 'How'd you hold that pitch?'"

"I said, 'Um, like this.' To this day, I don't know what made me hold the ball that way. Johnny just jammed the ball into my chest and said, 'Keep throwing it that way.' That pitch changed my career."

Hume enjoyed an 11-year major league career, and made the National League All Star Team in 1982.

Pitchers can be strange creatures, relief pitchers stranger still: high-strung, neurotic, insecure, blessed with short memories, cursed with short attention spans. Getting the best from pitchers required me to know who they were as well as what they threw. Pitchers came in three distinct types: (1) the pitcher I'd introduce myself to at the beginning of the game, make sure his mind was on his business and tell him I'd talk him through it; (2) the wired, Type A guy I had to pace like a Kentucky Derby winner. I'd watch his pitching mechanics, keep him in tempo and generally manage his game; (3) the guy who drove me crazy. I'd walk a mile, just making trips from behind the plate to the mound, to keep his head in the game.

To earn the trust that is vital in managing people, whether they're pitchers or workers on an assembly line, you have to show them you're in complete control. If they have questions, you've got answers, and every answer you have is aimed at making them more successful.

Another story: In 1969 I caught a game on Saturday night that lasted until about 1 a.m. I left the park and got back to my apartment around 2 a.m. and tried to get some needed rest since we had to report to the park at 10 a.m. I was a little tired. Did I say a little? I was in a stretch where I caught 54 games in a row without a day off.

Gerry Arrigo, a veteran left hander, was on the mound for us that day and owned a fair fast ball and a darn good curve. We were getting knocked around and Gerry was struggling a bit that day. His curve was by far his number one pitch, so I put down two fingers for the old bender, but he shook me off. I gave him two fingers again and got the same result. Once more I called for the curve and damn if he didn't shake that off. All right, then throw that mediocre fastball. Let me say that Gerry was in the majors because he had Major League stuff except for this day and I was just too worn out to argue. Why I did it? I'm not sure. But the pitch was up and away.

I reached out and caught it bare handed. The look on Arrigo's face was sheer shock. He just stared in and gave me the sign of the raisin heart. That's when you close your hand into a fist over your heart, meaning that you have shriveled up that big old grape of a heart. You stabbed me.

The Dodgers were the visiting team and when I heard the laughter coming from their dugout, I glanced that way, but they were all lying on the floor and couldn't be seen. I felt I was making the right decision when I called that pitch. I wanted Gerry to get that hitter out or for that matter any hitter he faced. My only concern was what was best for that pitcher.

Asked a few years later about the story, Gerry said it was his curveball, not his heater. I love that guy.

I studied opposing hitters. I knew who was slumping and who was hot. I was aware of situations. If we can't get the guy at the plate, can we get the guy standing in the on-deck circle? I knew which hitters were dangerous enough that walking them was a good idea. Some games, if my pitcher had five walks, I called for four of them. I knew which hitters had trouble hitting a certain pitch, delivered to a certain spot. I'd notice the way hitters stood in the batter's box.

It involved more than simply reading a scouting report. My pitchers had to know I was going to call the right pitch in the right situation. As Clay Carroll put it recently, "Johnny knew what a pitcher had, and when he wasn't giving it all he had."

I'd watch our pitchers in spring training. Is this guy consistently high with his fastball? Does that guy always bounce his breaking ball? What are his mechanics looking like when he's pitching?

I'd watch pitchers before games, in the clubhouse. Were they serious the day they were pitching? Were they making jokes? Did they tend to be nervous? How would I handle that during a game?

I knew our pitchers as well as they knew themselves. I'd take pitchers out to dinner, mostly to keep their confidence up. "Bury me with a little constructive criticism" was how Tom Hume put it. "Don't be afraid," I'd tell Hume. "Keep throwing it. If you're timid, you get beat."

Some pitchers I could put on auto pilot. Tom Seaver knew what he wanted to do and how he wanted to do it. When he pitched, I called the pitches he wanted to throw, not the ones I wanted him to throw. I rarely said a word to Seaver, so when I did, it was easy to recall.

On one of his first starts after he came over to Cincinnati from the New York Mets, Seaver started the game allowing two runs on four consecutive hits. I walked out to the mound, stuck the ball in his glove and said, "Are you trying?" Seaver growled, said if we scored three runs we'd win and told me to get my butt back behind the plate. We won, 3-2.

The most important thing a catcher can do for his pitcher is put down a sign asking for a pitch the pitcher has no doubt about. It's the equivalent of assigning an employee a task he understands completely. Not only how he is expected to do it, but also why.

After a few years, I had the advantage of being thought of as the best at my position and someone known for his ability to call a good game and handle a pitching staff. As Tom Hume put it, "Johnny was always very assertive, controlling the game. You knew that he knew what was going on. I rarely shook him off."

Some pitchers I let shake off the pitches I was calling. Gary Nolan shook me off constantly. Most of the time, he'd come right back to the pitch I called to begin with. I let him do that because I knew him well enough to know he could think a good game as well as pitch one. Also, with the amount of arm trouble he had over his career, there were days when throwing a certain pitch caused him too much pain.

Frank Pastore started one season winning seven of his first eight decisions. He allowed me to call the game. He kept winning, and began to think he knew how to pitch. It was in Houston and Frank's eighth or ninth start when in the third inning Frank shook me off. I called time, walked deliberately to the mound, slammed the ball in his glove and said, "Don't you ever shake me off again."

Pastore was a young guy who didn't know he didn't have the game figured out yet. I had to remind him.

Managing employees is no different. You allow a certain amount of dissent, if it comes from people who have proven to be reliable, productive workers. Trust works both ways. When Frank Pastore became as accomplished and productive as Tom Seaver, I'd let him call his own game.

It doesn't always go exactly the way you'd like. Nothing ever does. Heading into the sixth game of the 1975 World Series, the Reds led the Boston Red Sox three games to two. In the bottom of the ninth inning of a 6-6 game, the Red Sox loaded the bases with nobody out. I went to the mound to get things straight with our reliever, Will McEnaney.

"Ball hit to you, throw back to me," I told him. Then I called for a slider to the Red Sox hitter, Fred Lynn. McEnaney threw a fastball.

You work on signs beginning in March. This was October. I'm expecting the pitch to be on the outside corner against the left-handed hitting Lynn. It arrives down and in. I don't know if I'd have been able even to knock it down. Good thing Lynn was looking for a fastball and hit the pitch.

The ball went on a line toward our leftfielder, George Foster. Foster made the catch. Denny Doyle, the Boston runner at third base, tagged up and tried to score. His third base coach, Don Zimmer, had screamed "No, no, no!" as Foster caught the ball. In the din and excitement of a World Series game at Fenway Park, Doyle thought Zimmer said, "Go, go, go!"

Foster's throw and my tag completed the double play. I walked out to the mound, shaking with anger by what I'd just witnessed. "Jesus, Will, what were you doing?" I asked McEnaney. "That could have been the game right there. I asked for a slider. You crossed me up."

To which McEnaney, a typically flaky relief pitcher, replied, "Yeah, I guess I did. Sometimes, these things work out." He got the next batter out and we went to extra innings, in a game we'd lose eventually in 12, on Carlton Fisk's epic home run.

It's the exception that proves the rule. Catch every ball. Do it by knowing your employees, letting them know you're in it for them and by boosting their confidence at every turn.

Every workplace has its share of Clay Carrolls. It's up to you to make them productive. As Clay said recently, "I was down and out until I got to Cincinnati. Then I was up and in."

"DON'T WASTE A WORRY"

It's hard to have perspective when you're lying face down in the back of a school bus, feet hanging from the emergency exit. At that moment, when the wheels of the crashed and broken bus were still spinning, fear and tragedy filled the view. Given the grace and luxury of time, that outlook changes and matures.

The crash made me grateful for life and accepting of death. I became a fatalist at age 17. I learned not to waste a worry or an opportunity. Billy and Harold Dean were gone. The lessons of that day remain. They were never clearer for me than in September of 1972, when attitude and opportunity met at a sweet spot in time. I hit the biggest home run of my career with a spot on my lung that, for all anyone knew at the time, could have killed me.

Rumors of bad health can be worse than the real thing. It's the not knowing that has us walking the floor at 3 in the morning. If the tumor is malignant, at least we know. The knowledge is enabling. I didn't know.

Early every September, each Cincinnati Reds player had to take a physical. It included a chest X-ray. I took mine, felt perfect, and was ready to leave.

"We need to take another X-ray," the nurse told me.

OK. Fine.

Then: "We need another." Then, finally: "We need more X-rays."

"Why?"

"Just another look."

What the last look confirmed was a spot the size of a half dollar on my lung. "A shadow," they called it. That was a great metaphor, for anyone looking.

This was September of 1972. Both the team and I had rallied from a miserable 1971 to play like the dominant Reds team of 1970. Team general manager Bob Howsam had acquired second baseman Joe Morgan, pitcher Jack Billingham, centerfielder Cesar Geronimo and infielder Denis Menke from the Houston Astros. Howsam wanted a fast, line-drive hitting player for the artificial surface game we played at Riverfront Stadium. Morgan, a driven, moody player who had worn out his welcome in Houston, fit the description.

Howsam wanted a pitcher who could give him a

lot of innings. That was Billingham. He also wanted a speedy centerfielder who could get to the outfield gaps in right- and left-center fields. Enter Geronimo. Howsam had determined that while most players possessed running strides that were six feet long, Geronimo's measured eight feet. He could get to more balls.

Howsam was right about everything. After winning just 79 games in 1971, we won the National League West division by 10½ games. I rallied to win the NL home run title by hitting seven home runs in the last week of the season. In the meantime, doctors were still trying to identify the spot on my lung. They tested me for tuberculosis and histoplasmosis, a fungal infection. Finally, doctors performed a bronchoscopy. They fished a probe into my lungs and procured tissue samples.

I've always been a fatalist. If the bus wreck and my own car crash had taught me anything, it was when your time is up, it's up. Thinking about dying is no way to live.

So I tried not to think about the spot. I didn't waste a worry. That was something I'd spent my whole life saying to my mother. Whether it was my brother Teddy joining the Army, my brother William marrying young and starting a family or me leaving home at 17, Katy Bench worried enough for all of us.

I told her then what I believe now: Do what you can to affect an outcome. Use the knowledge of others. Be prepared for what comes your way. Adopt an attitude of inner conceit that says you're better than any situation you might face.

It all came together for me in the bottom of the 9th inning of Game 5 of the 1972 National League Playoffs. We were behind 3-2 to the Pittsburgh Pirates. Pittsburgh was three outs from its second consecutive World Series appearance.

The Pirates were the bullies of the league. Everything about them personified aggression. They slid with their spikes up, their pitchers brushed you back. They were the kind of guys you wanted with you in a biker bar. If you were a boxer, they were a puncher. They had us on the ropes.

I led off the 9th against Pittsburgh's best relief pitcher, Dave Giusti. Giusti didn't have a great fastball, but he threw a palmball, a sinker that tailed away from right-handed hitters. The palmball was so good, you couldn't wait for the fastball. I was waiting to hit when someone in the stands right behind me yelled my name. I ignored that kind of thing, especially in a pressure situation like the one I was in. Then he said, "Your mom wants to talk to you." I turned to see her in the seats next to the Reds dugout.

In the 3rd inning, I'd told someone in our dugout

I was going to hit a home run to make a difference in the game. Now, it was the last of the 9th, we were behind by a run and Katy Bench was asking me to notice her. As I did, she said, "Hit me a home run." At least that's how I recall it. She maintained her words were, "Do what you have to do."

I chuckled to myself. "I wish it were that easy."

I hit a Giusti fastball about 400 feet into the second-deck green seats in left field at Riverfront Stadium. It was foul, by about 15 feet. "Damn," I thought to myself. "That was the pitch."

Giusti ran the count to a ball and two strikes. My thinking then was just to protect the plate and not strike out. I wasn't looking for the palmball or the fastball. I was just up there reacting. I hit the 1-2 pitch into the lower deck in rightfield. The game was tied. The Reds won the game later in the 9th inning, on a wild pitch by another Pittsburgh pitcher, Bob Moose.

Some moments in life remain forever frozen and crystal clear. Age won't dim the recollection of me rounding the bases amid absolute delirium. I can still hear the sound. It was a moment everyone who has ever played a sport lives for. It was a moment every Reds fan who experienced it will never forget. The roars, the jumping up and down, the mobbing I got from my teammates when I thought I'd touched the plate. It was a moment of absolute perfection.

And I still thought about the spot on my lung. It was a devil companion, perched like a bad dream in the back of my mind.

Two months later, Dr. Luis Gonzalez made a 12-inch, horizontal incision under my right arm. He pried apart two ribs. Then he removed the tumor from the right lung's inner lobe. It was benign, caused by an airborne fungus called coccidioidomycosis, sometimes known as San Joaquin Valley Fever. I might have contracted it months earlier, playing in a golf event in the desert. No one knew for sure.

Until then, I lived with something that could have killed me, for all anyone knew. I thrived, because I didn't waste a worry.

It helped that the Reds were in a pennant race. After the disaster of '71, I'd learned not to assume success. I didn't take it for granted. I was determined to enjoy it. The adrenaline of September kept the devil companion in the background. Subconsciously, I might have thought that winning a World Series would be a great way to go out. I don't recall. "The shadow" stayed in the shadows.

I was prepared. I did what I could individually. I used the knowledge of the doctors. The spot was in their hands. My attorney and friend Reuven Katz had scoured the country seeking the best surgeon. I had confidence in Dr. Gonzalez.

I was also confident in myself, that if my baseball career had to end, I would still be fine. I'd played in two World Series, been rookie of the year, twice been named Most Valuable Player. I'd toured the world with Bob Hope. I was young. I could do something else.

I'd always known that baseball was a temporary destination, with its own Before and After. I was naturally curious, so I'd talk to gas station attendants as readily as CEOs. The same holds true today. No one is too good that he can't learn from someone else. It's like Sparky Anderson once said, to a Cincinnati TV sports anchorman:

"See that guy there, John Bench? He could have been anything he wanted." I've always believed that. I've never stagnated in my life.

A reporter asked me after the '72 season—which ended in a World Series loss to the Oakland A's, the Reds' second such defeat in three years—what I might do if I couldn't play baseball any longer.

"When I'm 35, maybe I'll run for president," I said.

Too often, we're held hostage by our worries and fears. Instead of attacking a project, we dread its immensity. The idea of actually attempting it freezes us. The inactivity only breeds more worry.

The only way to solve a problem is to do everything you can to fix it, and not to concern yourself with things you can't fix. If I have to go to court, I'm going to hire a lawyer, I'm not going to represent myself. Either I find a way to solve a problem, or I find someone who knows more about it than I. All I can do is all I can do. I don't waste a worry.

I played golf three weeks after the surgery. Dr. Gonzalez had applied a new technique to my operation. I was the first patient he used it on, in fact. The operation spared the muscles in my back, which allowed me to keep playing. I played another 11 seasons.

The doctor also said to me, "You'll never be the same player. You cannot be as good as you were." I said, "Just playing is enough."

Dr. Gonzalez was right. I still owned my inner conceit; I'd just become a little more human. Before the surgery, I could be expecting a pitcher's breaking ball and still be quick enough with the bat if he surprised me with a fastball. After the surgery, I couldn't quite get there. Some nerve that had been cut had slowed my reaction time just that much. A hundredth of a second makes all the difference when you're trying to hit a ball traveling 95 miles an hour from 60 feet, 6 inches away.

It didn't affect my legs, though, so defensively, I was as good as ever. And of course, my brain still worked. I knew, better every year, how to outthink hitters. I adapted and did what I could. It's a little like aging. I used to ski the black diamond trails. That became unrealistic, so I switched to the blues. Now, I'm 60 years old and my body's feeling the full effects of being a catcher, and I can't ski at all.

Ultimately, I know I've done what I could, about things I could control. I hit the biggest home run of my career while living with the fear and uncertainty of a spot on my lung. If you are prepared, willing to use the knowledge of others and you possess the inner conceit that says you're better than any difficult situation in which you find yourself, you can do the same.

"LET'S GO GET A CHEESEBURGER"

In 1971, I went from MVP to MDP, Most Valuable Player to Most Disappointing. I saw it happening in April and I let it happen all year. It was the worst year of my career. It would become one of the most useful years of my life.

It started in a nationally televised game against the Los Angeles Dodgers. Throughout my career in Cincinnati, the Dodgers were our most hated rival. We competed for the top spot in the National League West division standings almost every year in the 1970s. Whenever the Dodgers played a weekend series in Cincinnati, we could count on near-sellout crowds.

We prided ourselves on our professionalism and teamwork, from the way we looked (no facial hair allowed, sanitary socks at uniform height) to the way we played. If the Dodgers were L.A.—touched by Hollywood celebrity—we were Cincinnati, as middle America as a group of future Hall of Famers could be.

We enjoyed beating no team more than the Dodgers.

Once you went to Dodgertown, their spring training site in Vero Beach, Fla., you could see why the Dodgers were the Dodgers. All the players trained together. They were a family. An 18-year-old kid could walk into camp and see Sandy Koufax or Maury Wills and Steve Garvey and Davey Lopes. Young players saw how the stars behaved and prepared.

The Dodgers were glamorous. Maury Wills dated Doris Day. Steve Yeager did movies. They were also a little too smooth, a bit scripted in how they talked and acted. I always thought Bill Clinton was a Dodger. The Dodgers were so polished it could be hard believing they were sincere.

But we respected them, and we knew we had to beat them to get to October. If we didn't win, they did.

But there was something fundamentally different about 1971. I went to spring training worrying about our starting pitchers. My concerns were justified right away. We started poorly. A team that in 1970 prided itself on giving great effort every day developed a defeatist attitude. We were lethargic all year.

The year before, the Reds had won 70 of their first 100 games and cruised to a division title and a National League pennant. We dominated teams offensively. Our pitching staff was good, if overshadowed. In the midst of the dominance, cracks appeared, the biggest being the season-ending injury to a young all-star pitcher named Wayne Simpson. Simpson was 12–1 at the All Star break, injured his shoulder and wound up the season 14-2. I've never seen more explosive stuff, but his career would never be the same. That's another reason we should be prepared for life after baseball.

The 70-30 start gave way to a 32-30 finish and a five-game loss to the Baltimore Orioles in the World Series. Worse, we stood 'pat' in the offseason, judging from the 70-30 start more telling than the 32-30 end. We were wrong about that. I knew it as soon as I stepped in the batter's box that day in April.

The bases were loaded late in a one-run game, the sort of situation I'd thrived on since I was a six-year-old playing Little League. The Dodgers had a journeyman reliever named Pete Mikkelsen on the mound. Mikkelsen had a decent major league career, but I should have owned him in that situation.

I guessed with the bases loaded, the count full and the game close, he'd have to challenge me with a fastball and throw a strike. When Mikkelsen offered a screwball, I was the most surprised person in the park.

The ball came in at the knees. I was too stunned even to foul it off. I watched it for strike three.

I was amazed I could be so fooled I couldn't swing. I was absolutely astonished that in that situation, any pitcher would have the nerve to throw me an offspeed pitch and think he'd get it by me. But Pete Mikkelsen did just that.

I thought: "Is this how it's going to be all year? Will it go around the league that you can get me out without challenging me? What do I do about that?"

Not enough, as it turned out. In 1970, I hit 45 home runs and drove in 148. In '71, I hit 27 homers and had 61 RBIs. Ironically, I started well. I batted .312 in April, with nine home runs. The club finished the month 8-12. I started to feel as if nothing I did was good enough.

Instead of relaxing, I tried harder. I started trying to hit three homers in one at bat. I made the team's season-long funk my own. When things go negatively, you become part of the negativity.

On top of all of it, I was 23 and had never experienced losing. In fact, I'd been the nation's hero the year before. I'd toured overseas with Bob Hope, I'd worked the talk-show circuit. What later in life I would come to call my Inner Conceit had kicked into high gear. But until 1971, it had never been tested.

I failed the first test. I finished with a .238 batting average. I didn't hit a home run between Aug. 22 and Sept. 19. The team ended up 79-83, in fourth place, 11 games behind.

I wasn't alone in failure. The Reds organization

had failed, too, in not seeing the problems we would have with pitching in 1971. Management stood still and lost ground. I remember days that year when I went behind the plate and I just knew we couldn't score enough runs to overcome our pitching.

When you're calling pitches for pitchers you know can get people out, you have something to work with. We didn't have that in '71. No matter what I called, we didn't have the pitchers to make it happen. My approach became, "We can't do enough as a team, so I'm going to have to do more as an individual." As it turned out, I tried to do too much.

Then the boos hit.

Players can tell you the booing doesn't bother them, they tune it out, fans pay their money, they're entitled, etc., etc. They're lying. We all hear the boos, and they sting.

People will say to me, "You're a professional athlete making lots of money, booing shouldn't bother you, it comes with the territory." That's when I say, "OK, walk into your office and have four or five people boo you and see how you feel."

You expected it in other cities. I didn't like it there, either. I thought the people who booed were idiots, but I took it as a sign of respect. As Pete Rose explained it, "If they didn't care, they wouldn't boo." Fair enough. But I let the booing at home games affect me.

It was disheartening. I was coming off an MVP season, I'd been rookie of the year in '67. I'd shown I could play. By the first of May, I was getting booed at Riverfront Stadium. Some players used the booing as motivation. The great Ted Williams played his whole career "to shut the bastards up," as he put it.

Williams stayed within himself and trusted his talent. I tried too hard. Between the team's slump, my slump and the boobirds, I went into a shell. It was a combination of embarrassment at my own performance and my anger at those who so recently had cheered everything I'd done. I didn't go out much. When I did, it was only with a few, close friends. Even then, I'd see a fan after a game when I'd hit two homers and driven in five runs and he'd say, "I saw you pop out today."

The booing still affects me. To this day, I will say my best day in the game was the day I retired. I couldn't make any more outs.

The whole year was frustration and a mystery. I'd always prided myself on being the best I could be at whatever I tried. Further, when I wasn't the best, I'd work my way out of it. In 1971, for the first time in my life, the working didn't work.

Unlike other sports, baseball offers no rest between games. You can't spend several days or a week fixing what's wrong. The best and worst thing about the game is its everyday-ness. You're only as good as your next game. Baseball redeems and humbles, daily. The team and I got more of the latter in '71.

If you don't learn something from a year like that, you'll never be the person you can be. Losing is the next best thing to winning. But only if you understand why you lose. For the Reds and me, 1971 became the world's best learning experience.

I recall a conversation I had with my father after a Little League game we'd won. We'd upset a very good team. Their players reacted by crying. (Today, it'd be the parents doing the sobbing.) I asked my dad why the kids were bawling.

"They haven't learned to lose yet," he said. "Let's go get a cheeseburger."

That wasn't the first time Ted Bench would say that to me. When I was 6 and we could barely field a team—Ted had to drive house to house in his pickup, soliciting players—we lost much more than we won. Ted's reaction to every loss was the same:

"We'll get 'em tomorrow. Let's go get a cheeseburger." Eventually, we fielded teams that won championships. And we still got the cheeseburger.

This attitude has governed my whole life. In 5th grade, I made a C in penmanship. I knew then I wanted to be a major league ballplayer and when I was, I wanted my autograph to be perfectly legible. Even today, I get on former players who sign an autograph no one can read.

I spent hours practicing signing my name. And I never made a C in penmanship again.

My rookie year, I committed 15 passed balls. The next year, none. The first time I was behind the plate against the St. Louis Cardinals, Lou Brock led off with a double. Brock was arguably the fastest player in the league at the time. Being a cocky know-it-all kid, I decided I'd pick him off.

"Maybe he doesn't know about me," I said to myself.

Brock had a huge lead at second base. I threw down there, what I was sure would be an easy pickoff. Brock simply took third on the throw. He taught me a lesson I never forgot.

Lose and learn.

People say we have to be our own worst critics. I think we have to be our own best critics. I stagnated after 1970. I became satisfied. More, I assumed I could continue to improve while putting out the same effort. Reds management did, too. Look what it got us both in 1971.

Two weeks after the season, I went to the instructional league, where a coach named Lew Fonseca said to me, "Just allow your natural abilities to work."

By the spring of '72, we were ready to take

off again. We wouldn't land until we'd won three pennants and two world championships in the next five years. Gary Nolan's arm had come back. With Morgan at second, we had a Hall of Fame catalyst at the top of the order. In '72, Morgan stole 58 bases and scored 122 runs. Geronimo gave us a Gold Glove in center field. Billingham was one of the most underrated starters of his time. He won 19 games twice for us, in '73 and '74. Imagine the money Billingham would make today.

The trade brought the winning attitude back. We'd played poorly, we'd taken stock, we'd made the fix. Seventy-one was an aberration. We were still the Big Red Machine.

Bobby Richardson, the great second baseman of the New York Yankees, once said to me, "If what you did yesterday is big to you now, then you haven't done much today." You have to approach every day as if it's your first. The 45 homers I hit in 1970 meant nothing on that April day in 1971, when Pete Mikkelsen embarrassed me with a 3-2 screwball.

Question everything. Be your own best critic. Never think you've got it made. Between 1968 and 1970, I didn't have enough hours in my day to satisfy the requests of people who wanted a piece of my time. In 1971, the phone stopped ringing. It was a "didn't-you-used-to-be-Johnny-Bench?" feeling. I didn't like it. But from the '71 season, I'd learned the only way out was to be honest with and critical of myself, get over it, make the changes and move on.

If you're the head of a company, constantly evaluate who you are and what you're doing. You will make mistakes. The successful people learn from them, take them in stride and move on. The successful people get a cheeseburger.

I hit .267 for my career. I failed more than 73 percent of the time, and I was selected as the best catcher of the 20th century. And after April 1971, Pete Mikkelsen never fooled me on a full-count screwball again.

THE COMMON GOAL'S
THE BEST GOAL

After Doug Flynn got his first big league hit, Rose brought him his hat and glove at the end of the inning. Flynn was feeling special, then Rose said, "Congratulations, kid. You're only 2,500 behind me."

We took the time with those guys. We took them to dinner, we talked to them at the batting cage and in the outfield during batting practice. When Flynn started at second base, I'd tell him which players on the other team were likely to steal and which were likely to bunt in certain situations.

I even helped Flynn get his first major league home run. We were up 8-4 late in a game. Flynn was batting with a 3-1 count and runners at first and second. Sparky Anderson wanted him to bunt. I was sitting in the dugout next to Sparky and said to him, "Let the kid swing away." Flynn hit a three-run homer on the next pitch. We were languishing around .500 at the time. We went on to win 41 of our next 50 games.

The point is, Pete, Tony, Joe and I never big-timed our reserve guys. Bill Plummer was my backup. He had a good arm and was durable. He took bullpen catching seriously, so when he played, he knew our pitchers and what he could get out of them. He was prepared every day. We let him know how much we appreciated that.

The Big Four led by example. We kept our hair short, as per Reds policy. We wore our socks low, for the same reason. We were the first four players in the clubhouse every day. We were never too good to do all the little things that make the difference between a professional and someone who's taking up space. If we followed the letter, everyone else figured they'd better do it, too.

"They'd always mention us after games," Flynn recalled. "Johnny could hit a couple homers and if I had a hit or made a good play in the field, he'd tell the press about that first."

Doug Flynn could never be Joe Morgan. But he won a Gold Glove several years later, as a New York Met. Terry Crowley and Merv Rettenmund had distinguished big league careers. Rettenmund started for the Baltimore team that beat the Reds in the '70 Series. He and Crowley both played big roles for the '71 Orioles who won the American League pennant. They prepared every day as if they'd be needed to win a game that night. They would do just that.

The relationship among all 25 players in the Big Red Machine clubhouse was, as Flynn said, "one of the most remarkable things I've ever experienced." The dynamic between Pete, Joe, Tony and me was a little more complex. But whatever our differences, we all pulled together when we stepped on to the field.

As Joe Morgan put it in his book, "We were acutely conscious of how to keep our natural competitive rivalry within bounds." Morgan, for example, was an outstanding table tennis player. We had a couple of tables in the clubhouse, but Joe would never play Pete. He understood how competitive Rose was, and how angry Rose would get after Morgan beat him.

Morgan was the best ballplayer I ever saw. He could do whatever you needed to win. In 1972, his first as a Red, Morgan stole 58 bases and scored 122 runs. He could have stolen more, but he only took off when we needed a run.

Joe came to the Reds with a reputation as a moody player. If he was, we cured him of it. "Joe, you better watch out, you're going to step on that lip," Perez would say to him at the first sign of a pout. Morgan was as focused on winning as any player I've ever been around. He wrote in a notebook after every game, first thing. He noted the pickoff moves of pitchers, what pitches pitchers threw him in certain situations, mistakes he'd made and how he'd correct them.

Joe and Pete were linked by their absolute love of the game. They'd usually be the first two in the clubhouse each day, followed quickly by Tony and me. They'd clean their bats with rubbing alcohol, to remove the ball marks from the previous game. That way, they'd know instantly where bat met ball that night.

Joe and Pete played hard and with a baseball smartness not often seen. Pete taught Joe how to recognize in his first step out of the batter's box whether he could stretch a single into a double. Joe was suited perfectly to the hard, fast artificial surface of Riverfront Stadium. At the plate, he could slap balls through the holes. In the field, he could get to balls other infielders could not.

Pete Rose was simply obsessed with the game. He knew his stats. And yours. I'd hear that Pete and I didn't get along because I was jealous of Pete's popularity in Cincinnati, where he grew up. I laughed. Pete made my job easier on every level. He was getting 200 hits a year, so there was usually someone on base to drive in when I got up. It's a lot easier to reach 100 RBI when the people in front of you are getting 200 hits.

"You should hit .300," Pete once said to me.

"You hit .300," I said. "I'll drive in 100 runs."

Pete also liked dealing with the media, something I tolerated. The more Pete talked, the less Joe and I had to. We always appreciated Pete for that. Pete was brash about his goals and his skills. He wanted to be the first singles-hitter to make $100,000 and drive a Cadillac. Years later, while he was managing the Reds, Pete said he wanted selfish players on his team, because if they got theirs, everyone would benefit.

The most important gear in the machine was Tony Perez. As Joe Morgan wrote, "Tony could convert almost any situation to laughter, because his heart was so pure, his goals for the team so clear." Tony kept us from taking ourselves too seriously. There was nothing phony about Tony. We all respected him and trusted him completely.

Plus, the man was the best clutch hitter I ever saw. I can't tell you how many times I'd come back to the dugout after failing in a big moment and hear, "Don't worry, JB, I'll pick you up." More often than not, he was right.

When the Reds traded Tony after the '76 season—for Woodie Fryman and Dale Murray—I cried. Literally. I knew that was the end of the Big Red Machine. He meant everything to us, on the field and off. So genuine, so consistent. For 11 years in a row, he drove in at least 90 runs.

I recall one year, next to the last day of the

season, Tony had 89 RBIs. I was aware of the streak. There was a man on third and two outs. I was up, Tony was on deck. I fouled off several pitches, before taking the walk. Tony drove in the run, to keep his streak alive. "I know what you did," his wife Pituka said to me after the game.

He'd have done the same for me.

We genuinely liked each other. We looked forward to going to the ballpark, because we knew we were going to win and we enjoyed each other's company. We also got rid of the people who didn't fit. That's if we let them play for the Reds at all.

Sparky Anderson would consult the Big Four before recommending a trade to the general manager, Bob Howsam. If we didn't like the player or didn't believe he'd fit on our team, we'd veto him. If there was a guy available that we wouldn't like to have dinner with, he wouldn't be on our club.

Joe, Pete, Tony and I ruled the clubhouse, make no mistake. One spring, Sparky told the team, "I have one set of rules for you guys, and one set for them," pointing to the Big Four. "Their rules are, they have no rules." Nobody questioned us, because of what we'd accomplished already, but also because everyone understood our interest was in winning as a team.

We thought everyone on those great teams was indispensable, and we treated them that way. What you need to do, no matter who you are, is do your job the best you can. If the team wins, everyone benefits. Bill Plummer's World Series rings look the same as mine. Terry Crowley's postseason paycheck cashed the same, for the same amount.

Sparky's ability to manage people played a big role as well. Sparky took the time to know his players individually, so when he needed to motivate someone, he knew what made him tick. But much of the chemistry was internal, forged among players who respected each other and understood the common goal was the best goal.

I don't think it will ever happen in sports again. We celebrate the individual now. We glorify the I. Players' agents blow smoke at them, fill their heads with notions of greatness and entitlement, when little of it is justified or deserved. Great teams, in the true sense of the word, are rare. The New England Patriots come to mind. Who else?

If the Big Red Machine showed anything, it was the universal power of everyone rowing together, pulling the same oar, never letting egos, selfishness and petty jealousy overwhelm the overriding goal.

The Big Red Machine: It's a good nickname on many levels, both obvious and subtle. We were machine-like in the way we rolled over teams with our power and speed and ability to score. But we were also a perfect assemblage of parts, each part knowing its job and always prepared to perform it.

That's the legacy of the Big Red Machine. Any corporation can practice it. You don't have to be Tony, Joe, Pete and Johnny to make it work. You just need the mindset.

GET OVER IT

I didn't want to believe it happened. That moment, I didn't want to look at them. How does a 17-year-old die like that? I wanted to remove myself from that situation and the pain it was causing their parents, their friends and the school.

What do I do when someone close to me dies? How do I deal with a personal setback like the deaths of my friends when I was in high school?

How do you make sense of any of that? The answer is, there is no making sense of it. I lived. They didn't. I was lucky, that's all. The best way to acknowledge my good fortune is to honor their lives by living mine the best way I know how.

Get over it.

It's not a unique phrase, but it's among the most necessary. I'd heard it a million times before it finally stuck with me. Steve Gatlin, of the Gatlin Brothers of country music fame, was my caddie one day many years ago, at a charity event in Lake Tahoe. I'd hit several bad shots in just a few holes and was giving myself a good beating for them.

"Get over it," Steve said. "You have to hit another one."

We buried Billy Wiley and Harold Dean Sims a few days after the bus crash. We had an assembly at Binger High School, honoring their passing. I cried for the first time about something that didn't involve physical pain. A few days after that, we played another game.

Get over it. Get over the spot on your lung. Get over the 1970 and '72 World Series defeats. Get over the disastrous 1971 season in between. Three divorces, the deaths of your parents, the everyday setbacks and disappointments that can define our lives.

Get past them. It's not just a good suggestion. It's mandatory.

Callous? Only at first blush. When my dad died in 1991, I didn't even go up to see him in his casket. That wasn't how I wanted to remember Ted Bench.

If you don't get over it, what's the alternative? Pitying yourself? A friend of mine has a saying for that: "Get off the cross, we need the wood." Dwelling on tragedy? You doom yourself to reliving it. What kind of life is that?

It's like my high school friend David Gunter explains: "You can sit there and mope and feel sorry for yourself and your friends. Why did it happen to us? Why did it happen to them? It does sound callous, but you have to get over what happens in life. If you don't, life will bring you down."

"We had 17 in our graduating class," David said not long ago. "Imagine how close-knit we were. We dedicated the rest of the year to those two guys. It was a healing process, but we worked it through, partly by doing what we loved to do. What they loved to do, and that was play ball. You just have to force yourself to go forward."

"Getting over it" also means getting over yourself. My senior year, I was all-state in basketball. Only one other boy from Binger had made all-state in any sport. After I got the news, the first person I saw was a junior named Sandra Croy. I wanted to impress her. "Sandra, I just made all-state in basketball," I said.

"So what?" she responded. "Somebody had to."

I saw Sandra 15 years later and thanked her. "You taught me a valuable lesson: Never expect people to be impressed with who you are or what you've done," I said. That set a tone for my career and my life. To make a point, I've mentioned some of my accomplishments in this book.

Ted Bench died of heart failure at age 73. Katy Bench passed in 2004, at 83. I talk to both of them still. I'll be watching a golf tournament on TV, see an especially good shot and say, "How about that one, Dad?" Same with baseball. "Did you see that throw by that catcher? Just how you taught me. Throw it by your ear. Keep it on a line."

Anytime I'm ironing my clothes, I think of Katy, keeping my baseball uniforms crisp and pressed. I can be eating somewhere, an aroma will drift from another table, and I'll think of eating her roasts on Sundays, or her peach cobbler.

I live for them still, through what they taught me. Everything I do, I do according to the rules. I remember Katy telling my older brothers, Teddy and William, to go to the yard and cut a switch from a tree, so she could whip them with it after they'd misbehaved. I was a much better behaved kid than my brothers.

It comes up now in all areas of my life. A good example is the question I always get, after I've finished a speech or a round of charity golf:

"Does Pete Rose belong in the Hall of Fame?"

No, I say.

"I think he should be there."

You do? OK, I say. Then go home tonight and tell your kids that rules don't matter. That said, I still wish Pete Rose would recognize his problem with gambling and get the help he has needed.

I was inducted into the Hall of Fame in 1989. Ted Bench went with me. By the end of the weekend, it felt as if he'd been the one honored. My dad wanted to play professional ball, but life didn't allow it. He served two tours of duty in World War II, then came home to Oklahoma to work and raise a family. He was able to live vicariously through my career. I've given him a life of which I hope he'd be proud.

Ted Bench spent the Hall of Fame weekend introducing himself to the famous. I'd go to the lobby of the old hotel there, the Otesaga, and I'd have former players such as Pee Wee Reese, Ted Williams and Roy Campanella tell me, "I just met your dad."

When I gave my induction speech, I said, "I'd introduce you to my dad, but most of you have already met him."

I honored my parents by the man I became, through their love and devotion. Every day, I do what Ted did. I get up, do my job, take care of my family. When he died, I was able to get over it with that knowledge.

There is one especially instructive scene in the movie "Saving Private Ryan." Ryan, an old man half a century removed from serving in World War II, is visiting the American cemetery in Colleville Sur Mer, in Normandy above Omaha Beach. The sergeant who saved his life is buried there.

The dying words of Sgt. John Miller to John Ryan: "Earn this."

Fifty years later, Ryan gazes at Miller's headstone, then turns to his wife and asks, "Have I been a good man?"

Life is for the living. You're going to be dealt hands you don't know how to play. As a high school baseball team, we had no idea how we'd go on without two of our players, who were also our friends. In a little place like Binger, Okla., everyone knows everyone. My junior year, we won the state championship with 11 players.

When two in that group die, immediately you're numb with fear. What next? All you could do was play the next game. Overcome your grief by facing it. Deal with it by leading a life those you've lost would find admirable. Be a good man. Physically, Harold and Billy, Ted and Katy have all passed. They've never left me, though. They're very much a part of my life.

You've got to put on the gear and catch another game.

THE ONE IN THE MIRROR

I've tried to live all the suggestions I've made in this book. They have explained my successes and informed my failures. I've had professional and personal triumphs, each leavened with enough tragedy and failure to keep me humble. I've had a very good life.

But it wouldn't mean much if I didn't share it.

The wonderful little secret about doing for others is it makes you feel as good as it does them. If I neglected those less blessed than I am, all the successes would be hollow.

Leave it better than you found it. Make people better for having known you. You'll feel good about yourself, too. You'll like the person in the mirror.

I had lots of motivation for leaving home at age 17 to play professional baseball. At the top of the list was to make everyone who'd helped me proud. That extended from my parents to my junior high principal to my high school coach. I feared failing, because I didn't want to let any of them down.

In Binger, everyone knows you. If you're successful away from home, everyone lives vicariously through you. "What'd Johnny do today?" became the town's hottest topic, from the time I was a teenager playing Class A ball in Newport News, Virginia, until I retired in 1983, 17 years later.

How could I fail those people? As a kid, I'd be riding my bike or running through town, on the way home. I'd see a car pass by, with out-of-state license plates, and I'd think, "If those people only knew I was going to be a star in the big leagues." I became that star, but I never lost my small town-ness. It nurtured me then; it grounds me now.

When I was 12, my friend Jerry Scott and I trespassed into an abandoned house once owned by Native Americans. We took some things from the house. Beads, mostly. Some jewelry.

The next day, I'm in the front yard, tossing a ball, when I see dust flying on the dirt road by our house. It's the Caddo County sheriff, Troy Massey. My dad had heard what I'd done and called Troy, who proceeded to scare me straight for the rest of my life.

"That's a federal offense," the sheriff said. "I'm going to have to take you down to Anadarko, fingerprint you, take your picture and send all of it to Washington, where you'll have a record the rest of your life. Unless you promise you'll never do it again."

"I'll never do it again."

The worst of it wasn't the fear of the sheriff or the whipping I got. It was the look in Ted Bench's eyes when he discovered what I'd done.

Binger fostered a sense of place in me. From that grew my notions of responsibility and accountability. I've been lucky to have met so many people who have reinforced those notions, starting with my father.

He spent Saturdays coaching baseball games, driving to baseball games or sitting with me on the couch, watching the major league game of the week. Talk about someone who lived his dreams through his youngest son. How could I let him down?

Hugh "Sosh" Haley coached junior high baseball. He was also the principal and math teacher at the school. No one taught me more about giving than Sosh. He never did anything big. He was just always there, if I needed a ride to a game or a hot dog afterward. Sosh made me feel special just by being Sosh. Anybody can do that. The small gestures are always the best, because they're the most heartfelt.

So many others have touched me with the same message. I spent 12 days in 1970 touring the world on a USO trip with Bob Hope. I met him in Burbank, California, where the troupe was rehearsing. Hope acted like we'd been friends our whole lives. It was like being back in the clubhouse and sitting at my locker.

The man had no ego. Bob Hope was already Bob Hope. All he cared about was putting on the best show he could for the troops. To do that, he needed everyone on the trip to be as good as he or she could be. He did that by making all of us feel like stars, and by having his writers give us some of the best lines.

We flew from California to England, Germany, Greece, Thailand and Vietnam. He was always upbeat and prepared, with a humility that brought everyone together. He knew all the generals' names. He never missed a line. Whoever walked out with him on that stage was the most important person in the world. If Bob Hope could handle everything with grace and humor, who were we to argue?

And the looks in the eyes of the soldiers during those shows! I'm this 23-year-old guy. I've just been named the National League MVP, yet I'm sheepish and feeling a little guilty, thinking I should be fighting the war, not playing a game. At least until thousands of soldiers thanked me on that trip, for giving them something from home to hold on to.

I knew then that doing for others would be as rewarding as anything I could do for myself. Arnold Palmer reinforced that. Arnold was Bob Hope on a golf course: Surpassingly talented, equally humble, forever willing to give of himself. Arnold never wanted to disappoint anyone.

Arnold knew everyone and treated everyone with the same respect. He understood his obligation to golf, and it didn't matter who needed a minute of his time, Arnold was always there to give it. It wasn't surprising that during his last competitive round at the U.S. Open, at Oakmont, Pa., in 1994, marshals at every hole knew Arnold personally or had a personal story about him to tell. He has a way of making everyone feel comfortable.

I've played with him many times in charity events. To say I've learned from him doesn't begin to describe it. The whole Arnold Palmer package—the integrity, the humility, the personal touch—is easy to see, harder to emulate. What sticks with me, though, is his sense of responsibility to those who made him who he is, from corporate CEOs to volunteers at golf events. He never fails to say thanks. I've always tried to do the same. If I've missed thanking a volunteer at a golf event in which I've played, I apologize.

I've learned to notice the joy other people take from what I've done. I've learned to slow down that extra second, to glimpse the gratitude in their eyes. It's one of the best things I can do for myself.

I can be standoffish. I do not like people who expect me to do something for them, as if I owe them.

I admit that. Don't expect an autograph from me if I'm eating in a restaurant or reading at an airport gate. When it comes to flying, I'm the last one on the plane and the first one off. I rarely speak.

When I enter a room, often before or after a speaking engagement or a charity golf event, I'm usually uncomfortable, because I know everyone is there for an autograph. But when you're busy signing hundreds of autographs, you rarely interact with anyone. I'm there to converse and inform...not to sign a scrap of paper that as often as not ends up on eBay.

I'll ask to pose for a picture first, or I'll tell people that I'll sign later. Now, let's talk.

I hope along the way, I've built bridges. I know people have made special trips to Binger, because that's how I still define myself and introduce myself to others. I'm not from Cincinnati, or Palm Springs or Naples, Fla., even though I have homes in those places. I'm from Binger, Okla., and carry proudly everything that means, from the hard work to the personal responsibility to the pride we take in each other's achievements.

As this is written, we are in the planning stages of the Johnny Bench Hall of Fame and Museum, which will be built in Binger or Oklahoma City.

Nothing has brought me more joy than the Johnny Bench Scholarship Fund. I started it upon my retirement in 1983. The Reds kicked it off with a $20,000 donation; Major League Baseball added $5,000. It's up to more than $2 million now. We gave out $97,000 worth of scholarships in 2006, to more than 80 kids from Binger and the Cincinnati area.

I started a college fund because I didn't get to go to college. At 17, I took the Reds' signing bonus. Days after high school graduation, I was on a plane to Tampa. I didn't get my four years to come of age in college. Every year, I get thank-you notes from the recipients.

I've never taken the time to get to know them, though. I didn't want to make them feel as if they owed me anything but their good work in the classroom. We're coming up on 25 years, so I might have to check in on some of them. Just to see their joy.

I do get those looks occasionally. They let me know what I've done means something. I'll be in an airport and a Vietnam vet will thank me for appearing in DaNang with Bob Hope. I'll be at a speaking engagement and a middle-aged man will tell me he was in Riverfront Stadium as a kid in 1972, when I hit the home run off Dave Giusti.

It's a small thing, really, making others feel good about themselves. Building bridges isn't the effort it seems. And the reward? It makes you feel so good, you almost feel selfish.

MY VOWELS FOR SUCCESS

Binger, Oklahoma, July 1953. White heat owns the backyard of the little house, shimmering off the wilted grass. Dad will be home soon from delivering propane all over Caddo County. Mom is in the yard, hanging clothes on the line. Dinner aromas—roast or chicken—glide from the open kitchen window. The world is still with certainty.

Wham!

William Bench, my older brother by five years, has just thrown an evaporated milk can from 40 feet away. I've swung a bat—half a cracked Louisville Slugger sawed down the middle from barrel to handle—flat side facing out—and sent the can flying toward the shed. If you hit it over the old shed you had a home run. Yes. It is gone. Another homer for the next Mickey Mantle. I am 6 years old.

Whap!

If we don't have a can, or if the can becomes too small and hard from the hitting, we roll up a gob of friction tape to regulation baseball size and we hit it with a bat studded with tacks, so the tape ball doesn't stick to the bat. I reprise my Mantle routine. Then, if it's Saturday, I plop myself down on the couch in the living room, where my dad is waiting to watch the "Baseball Game of the Week."

We share half a gallon of ice cream. Ted Bench tells me about the players on the TV. I tell him he'll be watching me someday.

To begin this book, I explained what I called the Vowels of Success, my way of remembering the traits I've needed to achieve. I asked you while reading to think of your own vowels. I've done the same over the years. Here are my five best:

A C H I E V E

Very few people in life set a goal early on and achieve it. If you are lucky, you know early on what you want to do. That's where the luck stops and you take over.

Achieving is nothing so much as having a goal and a path to reach it, and walking as straight as you can until you get there. When I was $3\frac{1}{2}$, I was watching the game of the week with my Dad on our black-and-white TV when the announcer said "now batting the next superstar, the switch hitting centerfielder from Oklahoma, Mickey Mantle." I looked at my Dad and asked, "You can be from Oklahoma and play in the Major Leagues? That's what I want to be." Dad told me that catching was the quickest way to the big leagues and what the big leagues needed. Dads are very smart. I wanted to be the best at everything I did, whether it was baseball, basketball or signing my name. I don't think you can have a problem with that. It's called pride.

I had ability. Everyone has ability. What separated me was my willingness to work. I earned what I came to own. I still have scars on my hands, from catching the jagged, evaporated milk can in the backyard.

After the great year I had in the 1970 season, and the poor '71 season, I went to the Instructional League. Talent without work is a lyric without a melody.

Life is dull to those who are satisfied. Bob Hope was 87 years old in 1990, and still entertaining U.S. troops in Iraq during Operation Desert Storm. Arnold Palmer might have stopped playing competitive golf, but he didn't vanish. He still oversees a business empire launched by the brilliance of his golf game and the force of his personality. Successful people believe there is more to be done.

Find your talent and examine it to its fullest. Test it and stretch it. Use it to make yourself and others better people.

EMPLOYABILITY

Would you hire yourself? Consider your resume. Update it in your mind. Is it good enough?

I pose that question to every group I speak to. It's usually in the middle of the speech. Invariably, it silences the room. Everything just stops. People begin to self-evaluate. Am I good enough? How can I be better? If you're not asking yourself that question often, you're not getting ahead.

I like people who challenge me mentally. I like talking to folks who can teach me things. My friend Tom Devlin started Rent-A-Center with nothing but an idea and a willingness to work. Anyone can do that.

Devlin says about me, "I know I can always depend on you," and he's right. I'm reliable. In 1968, my rookie year, I played in 154 games. In 1970, the year we won the NL pennant, I appeared in 158 games. In '74, it was 160, while playing the most physically demanding position in baseball. (When I wanted a "rest," the Reds played me at first base, third base or the outfield.) That is unheard of today. Sparky Anderson knew he could count on me.

Speaking of Sparky, he knew how to be employable. Anderson filled his coaching staff with bright men and his team with stars. Sparky was a brilliant baseball man, yet what made him effective was, he knew what he didn't know. He was able to take the advice of others. Early in my career, Sparky trusted me enough to take my advice during games, especially when it came to making pitching changes. Sparky wasn't a great manager when he took over the club in 1970. He learned on the job. He grew. He updated his resume constantly. He never stopped wanting to be better.

Surround yourself with people whose ideas you embrace, whose opinions you trust, whose values you admire. Don't try to achieve alone. It doesn't work.

Apply this to everything you do and all that you are. How's your resume as a parent, a husband, a wife, a friend? Are you "employable" in those areas? Take responsibility for who you are and who you want to become. Don't blame others when you fall short.

I established The Johnny Bench Scholarship Fund with employability in mind. I want bright, ambitious kids to have a chance to learn and give back some of what they know. Recently, I've asked that more of the money go to kids seeking vocational-technical training. I value people who can wire a house or lay a pipe as much as I do those who excel in white-collar jobs. My dad never went to college. He was too busy serving two tours of duty in World War II and then raising a family.

INNER CONCEIT

In March 1968, I was a 19-year-old rookie catcher with a major-league arm. Already, the veterans were talking about my ability to throw and my willingness to show off that skill.

In a spring training game that year, the Reds were playing the Kansas City Athletics. Rick Monday led off first base. Two years earlier, the Athletics had taken Monday with the first pick in the entire amateur draft. The Reds had picked me in Round 2. I'd made up my mind I was going to show off my arm, by picking Mister Top Draft Pick off first base. Plus, Monday had a big lead. His cockiness galled me. I could throw out anybody.

My throw to first sailed so high and wide off the mark, it reached the right field wall on one hop. Rick Monday ran all the way to third base. He had to be chuckling inside.

I picked him off third after the next pitch.

I was cocky, no question. There's nothing wrong with that, as long as it's directed properly. It's also a great motivator. Cocky people work hard to keep from looking foolish. Don't let your attitude write checks your ability can't cash. I preferred to see it as Inner Conceit, which, as I said before, is nothing more than knowing you're better than any situation.

I won 10 Gold Gloves as a catcher, but I'm not sure I ever led the league in fielding percentage. The Inner Conceit led me to take chances, to make throws other catchers wouldn't attempt. As a rookie in 1968, the older pitchers on the Reds staff called me the Little General, for my habit of taking charge of a game.

As a catcher, I believed I could throw anybody out. As a hitter, I took great offense whenever a pitcher got me out. Early in 1968, I faced Jim Bunning for the first time. Bunning would go on to pitch for 17 years, win 224 games and be elected to the Hall of Fame.

After Bunning popped me up with two runners on base, I slammed my helmet and stood at the top of the dugout steps, screaming. "You'll never get me out again." My teammate Lee May sat on the bench, laughing. "What are you gonna do, rookie?" he asked. "Quit?"

I also got into it early that year with our shortstop, Leo Cardenas. One job of a catcher is to make sure his players are in the proper places defensively. Cardenas was out of position. From behind the plate, I motioned him to slide over a step. He didn't. I did it again. Still, he didn't move.

After the game, Leo came up to me in front of my locker. Back then, if you'd been in the major leagues a certain number of years, they gave you a card recognizing your service time. Cardenas was in his 9th season. He flashed his card in my face.

"Rookie," he said, "when you get one of these, you can tell me where to play." Cardenas might have had a point. By '68, he'd already been an All Star three times and won a Gold Glove. I was a 20-year-old kid. Still, the Inner Conceit had an answer for Leo Cardenas.

"Next time," I said, "just move when I tell you."

None of it would have mattered if I hadn't studied hitters and situations and been proven right over and over. It wasn't an accident. To reach a point where your Inner Conceit is justified and rewarded takes years of practice.

In the decisive Game 5 of the 1972 NL playoffs, I sensed before the game I'd be put in a crucial situation and I knew I'd come through, because I'd prepared for it and done it before. I knew Pittsburgh reliever Dave Giusti would throw me his palmball in that situation, because I'd studied how Giusti pitched. I knew I could hit the palmball because I'd spent years learning to hit breaking pitches.

It all came together as the ball sailed over the right field wall. It was the biggest hit of my life. I was ready for the moment.

Confidence comes down to believing in yourself. Believing in yourself comes from putting yourself in important spots and doing the job, again and again. Strive to be better than the situation and the Inner Conceit will follow.

OPPORTUNITY

Opportunity comes dressed in overalls and looks like work. Movie producer Samuel Goldwyn said it best: "The harder I work, the luckier I get." PGA Hall of Fame golfer Gary Player borrowed the phrase. It served him very well over a long and distinguished career.

Opportunity isn't handed to you often. It's up to you to seize the day. Develop the Inner Conceit that allows you to take chances and maximize opportunity. Don't say no, even if the job seems insurmountable. Catch every ball. I'm a kid from a small town who has traveled the world and had a sitting president, George W. Bush, attend my 60th birthday party.

I've eaten dinner at the White House and played golf with Arnold Palmer. I've hosted television shows and been a network TV analyst on World Series broadcasts. What if I'd said no?

Catching is a physically demanding, exhausting job. After a season catching, all you really want to do is lie on a beach somewhere. I could have said no to Bob Hope in 1970, and not seen half the world entertaining troops. When I was asked to play golf in celebrity events, I could have decided to rest my soreness instead of punish it more. Maybe then, I wouldn't have met Palmer.

I wasn't very good on TV, but the talk shows and the networks gave me the opportunity to get better. If I hadn't taken it, I wouldn't be doing the speaking I'm doing now. If I'd decided sleeping in or watching TV was more important than taking Dom Zanni up on his offer to work on hitting curveballs, where would I be today?

Life rarely offers you more than a chance. It's up to you what you do with it.

USE

I reach out to my friends. Remember the Lifelines chapter? I live my life that way. Business question? Maybe I'll reach out to Tom Devlin with a phone call or a text message. Legal issue? My attorneys Reuven Katz and Mark Jahnke get contacted.

I reach out to my dad's memory. How would Ted handle this? If someone wants to talk about playing catcher, people generally reach out to me.

When I was still playing, I'd recall the advice of the late Reds slugger Ted Kluszewski: "Get your hands started." I could always summon Ted Bench, who wanted to play pro ball but life got in the way, so he settled for playing on Sunday afternoons. My dad swears he once got a hit off Satchel Paige, when Paige's team passed through Oklahoma on a barnstorming tour.

"Watch the ball past the pitcher's ear," he'd say.

At golf tournaments, I've been known to go to the range and just watch. "Aren't you going to hit balls?" someone might ask.

"I'm hitting balls right now. Mentally," I'd say. I'd be watching Palmer, Jack Nicklaus and Lee Trevino.

Never delude yourself into thinking you have all the answers, or even just the answers you need. Be available to the wisdom of others. Be humble enough to accept it. Life is better when lived with an open mind.

I was on the driving range at a tournament several years ago, mentally hitting balls, when a voice startled me. "C'mere," the voice said. "Tell me what I'm doing wrong." I watched Arnold Palmer hit a few golf balls. "Open your right foot up," I offered. "You'll have a better turn."

This felt something like telling Picasso how to paint.

THEIR VOWELS FOR SUCCESS

Arnold Palmer, Golfing Legend

Attitude—Your success is often determined by your attitude. If you think you are beaten, then you are. If you truly know in your heart that you are going to succeed, more often than not, you will.

Effort—The outcome of every endeavor is a product of the amount of effort you put into it. I'm a firm believer that there is nothing you can't accomplish if you put enough effort toward the task.

Integrity—I have found that the most successful people are those who have integrity. At the end of the day, you need to look at yourself in the mirror and decide if you were honest with others and, equally important, yourself. If you can't be proud of your own actions, others won't.

Obstacles—Life always presents obstacles, but it is those obstacles and how you choose to overcome them that not only define your character but also teach you the life lessons you need to succeed in the future.

Understanding—It is very important to understand not only what is going on in your own life but perhaps even more important to understand what others are doing and why they are doing it. It will make you a better citizen in your community.

Tom Seaver, Hall of Fame pitcher

Attitude

Excellence—Express enthusiastic energy while always striving for excellence.

Independence—Be an independent thinker in forming your own creative, positive and innovative ideas.

Opportunity—Look for opportunities to help your family, friends, and others.

Understanding—yourself and others.

Joe Morgan, Hall of Fame second baseman

Aggressive—Once you identify your goals, don't wait for something to happen. Don't be shy about striving.

Education—The quality of your life is directly related to the quality of your education.

Interest—Take an interest in those around you. Not just yourself. Help them reach their goals.

Obligation—We are obligated to carry on the

traditions of our parents and make life better for everyone.

U–You are in charge of your own destiny. You decide who you are.

Gary Carter, Hall of Fame catcher

Assertive–To gain respect and be a leader, you must exert your personality.

Enjoy–We have to be happy in what we're doing to be the best at it. When the joy in what you do is gone, it's time to move on.

Ideas–It's amazing how far our country has come just by utilizing the brain.

Obligation–There is a responsibility in everything we do. You can ask no more than to look in the mirror and see someone who has given everything he has to whatever he tries.

Understanding life's purpose–I realized I was blessed with athletic talent but I understood nothing would be handed to me. What I put into it was what I was going to get out of it.

Bobby Bench, Johnny's son

Ardent–Show enthusiam for and be passionate about what you are doing.

Effort–Dedicate the time.

Integrity–The ends only justify the means if the means are just.

Optimism—"Why do we fall? So we can learn to pick ourselves back up."—Batman Begins

Unique—You have to stand out from the crowd, show something that others can't.

Shannon Miller, gold medal Olympic gymnast

Action—Many will talk about how they will succeed; few turn that talk into action and truly meet their goals.

Enthusiasm—When you start each day with enthusiasm, passion and joy, progress is inevitable.

Imagination—Never limit yourself. Create innovative ways to reach your goals.

Opportunity—Look for it in every mistake and failure.

Underestimate—Never underestimate yourself.

Bob Knight, Hall of Fame basketball coach

A#?holes—Avoid them. Be aware of who they are.

Extra—Always do more than is required of you. Extra concern for what you do will put you ahead of the multitudes who do only what they have to do.

Industriousness—Those who accomplish the most, work the hardest to do the most. Identify what has to be done, then do it.

Obstacles and *Opportunities*—Life is full of both. Recognize each. Work harder to overcome obstacles and be quick to identify opportunities. Also, nothing is more vital to success than being observant. Being observant of people and circumstances puts you ahead of the multitudes who have no clue as to whom they are watching and what they see.

Understand the rules of the game—Apply extra effort in all you do. Be industrious, recognize opportunities and understand the rules.

Bill "Bones" Slifer, CEO Watersaver
Approach—life's challenges with a great attitude.
Exercise—your brain every day.
Initiative—Take it every day, to make one person smile.
Observe—what goes on around you.
Unimaginable—success occurs when you work smart and treat people with respect.

Gary McCord, former PGA Tour pro and current TV analyst
Act like you know what you're doing.
Eliminate negative mental thoughts.
Invent ways to have fun.
O—Stay loyal to your circle of friends.
U—You are the man or woman. Believe it.

Lauren Bench, Johnny's wife
Adventurous—Be open to new things.
Energetic—Be energetic in mind, body, and spirit.

Inquistive
Outside the box—Think and act outside what is
expected of you.
Unwavering—Be steadfast in your beliefs.

**Dale Petroskey, president of the Baseball
Hall of Fame**
Accountability—Your work ethic and decisions
about how you spend your time will determine how
successful you are, and your integrity will determine
your reputation.
Enthusiastic—If you love what you're doing, your
enthusiasm will rub off on others.
Interested and *Interesting*—Successful people are
interested in others, asking them questions and
learning from them.
Original—Successful people understand everyone is
unique. Every situation requires original thinking,
perhaps drawing on lessons from the past, but
applying those lessons to the current situation with an
original twist.
Understanding—The world is made up of 6 billion
individuals. Successful people can put themselves in
the shoes of others.

Kathy Ireland, Lifestyle Designer
Anticipation—Keeping your eyes on the horizon and
your nose to the grindstone.

Empathy–Think of others. Realize we have a unique set of circumstances that brought us where we are today.

Insurance–Hope for the best. Plan for the worst.

Others–Put others before yourself.

Understand–Seek to understand rather than be understood.

Bob Castellini, principle owner and CEO, The Cincinnati Reds

Awareness of self

Energized

Integrity, Insatiable

Organized

Upbeat

Bob Wright, former president of NBC

Ambition–The drive you need to succeed.

Expertise–A skill you bring to the table that makes you valuable.

Integrity–Without it, any personal accomplishment is worthless.

Opportunity–Seize it when it comes.

Undeterred–Nothing truly worthwhile comes without persistence and hard work.

Reuven Katz, Johnny Bench's friend and attorney

Be *Accountable* and *Available*.

Energetic—To approach any matter with less than full energy is asking for failure.

Inquisitive and *Indefatigable*—The best way to learn is to study, observe and ask questions.

Optimistic—If one expects success, one is much more likely to succeed.

Unselfish—Take yourself out of a situation and work for the good of others. Your perspective will be much broader.

Randy Owen, lead singer of "Alabama"
Aggressive
Energetic
Intensity
Organized
Undaunted

Miller Barber, former PGA Tour pro
Attitude
Excel
Integrity
Outlook—Always be positive.
Understand your responsibilities.

John Selberg, Friend
Ask
Energy

Imagination
Optimism
Unique

Tom Devlin, Devlin Enterprises
Ability to adapt and to change.
Empower yourself and others.
Impossible–Know that it is attainable.
Obligation–Honor your obligation to work and family.
Understand you are only as good as the people
you hire.

**Clayton Cole, head golf professional, Cherry Hills
Country Club, Denver, Colo.**
Attitude sets the tone for all success.
Excellence will follow.
Innovation will occur.
Outstanding performance will result.
Underscoring the value of attitude.

Steve Gatlin, The Gatlin Brothers
Adversity–Everyone faces adversity. It doesn't matter
if you are rich or poor, black or white, famous or not,
troubled times happen in all our lives. Your quality
of life largely depends on how you handle adversity.
When adversity hits me, I try to "just keep on singing."
Eternity–Everything we do has an eternal sequence.

We are here only a short time and as I grow older, seeing my kids get married, soon to have babies, I realize, life is short, but eternity is forever. That's why my relationship with my God is very important to me.

Invest—It is important to always invest our money in the right places but more importantly to invest my time, attention and energy in my family. I am blessed with the best wife in the world and three beautiful daughters. They are my life.

Opinion—Always remember there is a difference between "opinion" and "fact." Allowing people to have an opinion that may differ from mine only makes me stronger. I try to see and understand where they are coming from. I don't always have to agree with that point but not considering it would be very closed-minded and not healthy. Plus, in the long run, if I disagree it has given me the opportunity to strengthen my view.

Up—Always look up. Things will always get better. Going through tough times is part of life but they will always pass. Looking toward a heavenly Father and realizing that He is in control, helps one get through those tough times.

Rudy Gatlin, The Gatlin Brothers
Attitude—Turn the other cheek. Take the High Road.

Stay above the fray. We're all called to a higher calling for our lives...Be honest, trustworthy, slow to anger.

Eternity–When it all seems to be going south, thinking about our Eternal home seems to ease the pain and suffering somehow.

Integrity–We're not much if don't have any. People knew what kind of person I was before they got to know me simply if they knew my dad, Curley Gatlin.

Obedience to God and the Golden Rule.

Understanding–Don't be so hard on others, we don't know the whole story and they are probably doing the very best they can under the circumstances. Forgive as we have been forgiven.

Reggie Jackson, Major League Baseball Hall of Fame Slugger, #44, "Mr. October"

Efficiency and *Excellence*–Study your direction and path to completion. Make sure that you are focused on the excellence of the production of the finished product.

Integrity and *Intelligence*–Quality and brilliance throughout the making of the product and your path of pursuit.

Original–Be true to your original thoughts and your desires to succeed. Recognize that you have probably formed your final ideas with some input from others.

Understand who you are and where you are headed, who the end user will be and where it fits in the marketplace. Cost and practicality.

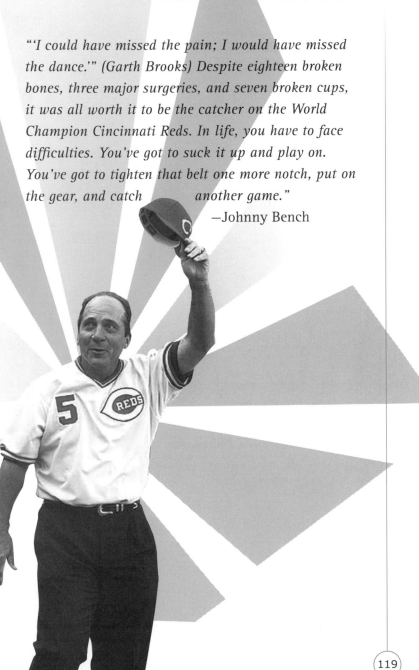

"'I could have missed the pain; I would have missed the dance.'" (Garth Brooks) Despite eighteen broken bones, three major surgeries, and seven broken cups, it was all worth it to be the catcher on the World Champion Cincinnati Reds. In life, you have to face difficulties. You've got to suck it up and play on. You've got to tighten that belt one more notch, put on the gear, and catch   another game."

—Johnny Bench